Self 1
for Busy,
Intelligent
Women

Liz Keaney

57 Ways to be KIND to your

Body, Mind and Soul

ISBN:1492244929
ISBN-13:978-1492244929

DEDICATION

To John. My Soul Warrior.
Health, Joy and Abundance x

CONTENTS

ACKNOWLEDGMENTS

Big thanks to the Warrior Women within the
#Kindnesscode Community.

We WILL make the 'dreamsdatabase' real.

Namaste.

Self Kindness for Busy, Intelligent Women

How to use this Book

There is a new tip for every week plus some extra. Simply start at the beginning or open the book randomly and select one tip at the start of each week. Take one tip for seven days and build it into your awareness and lifestyle. After 7 days you will have embedded a new way of mastering your mind, healing your body or connecting to your soul.

Chapter 1

<u>BE KIND TO YOUR BODY</u>

YOUR BODY has the ability to tolerate amazing amounts of stress and disrespect. You'll only become aware of how much is 'enough' when you start to feel less than vibrant or your body starts screaming with symptoms of ill health.

Don't wait for the screams - start taking steps to be kinder to yourself. After all, your body is the house you live in.

1

Give it some respect!

Now I'm sure this doesn't apply to you, but many people prefer to show more love and kindness to their vehicle than their body.

Self kindness begins with self respect; filling your body with high grade fuels. These include plenty of natural foods; vegetables, fruits, legumes, nuts and seeds. Sugar and processed grains such as white bread, packet cereals, white rice, white pasta and convenience foods are low grade fuels that rob your energy and exacerbate stress. Try making some small changes; swap a few of your sugary foods, processed grains and convenience foods for natural foods. Get into the habit of doing this every day and watch your body go the distance.

2

A well used door doesn't get rusty hinges!

Take time to move your body. It doesn't have to mean expensive gym memberships, gruelling workouts or sweaty Lycra. Find something you enjoy doing. How about walking? It's free and you get the benefit of listening to the birds and seeing great stuff at the same time. Walk with a friend and you can natter too. Save the cost of paying to go to an exercise class and put a fiver in a tin every time you walk. At the end of each quarter treat yourself. You'll have enough money to buy yourself a pamper treatment or an item of new clothing. You are worth it.

3

Your stomach doesn't have teeth.

Count how many times you chew food before you swallow. How about trying to slow it down? Chew at least ten times before you swallow. Food eaten too quickly is often the cause of digestive discomfort such as bloating, indigestion and heartburn. In the long term, undigested foods rot (like compost) inside you. Your body will struggle to let go of the unwanted toxins this compost attracts and will make you feel sluggish and zap your energy.

4

Eat consciously

Do you really taste your food or are you mindlessly munching away? How about trying to do doing nothing else while you are eating? This means not watching the telly, being on Facebook or reading the paper. Research shows eating consciously induces feelings of fullness more easily, resulting in less likelihood of overindulgence.

5

Eat regularly

Do you ever skip meals thinking it will help shed unwanted weight? Sorry to disappoint you but for most people this strategy has the opposite effect. Missed meals slow down metabolism which encourages weight gain. Missing meals also contributes to low energy, bad mood and headaches. Eat food regularly to keep your energy levels up and metabolism running smoothly.

6

You are worth it

Life is busy and stressful enough. It can be a challenge to take time out – but aren't you worth a lunch break? Busy people seldom make time to have a break, but did you know eating on the go contributes to additional stress in the body? Your body will find it less easy to digest food if you are eating 'on the go' and undigested food will add to existing stress. Even ten minutes is better than nothing. I guess you are worth that?

7

Check your sugar intake

Do you fall prey to frequent coughs, colds, illness or do you feel tired all the time? If so, check your sugar intake. Sugar competes with Vitamin C in the body and too much sugar can lower immunity. Be aware, sugar is often added to foods that don't even taste sweet! It's also added to flavoured waters and typically canned drinks are overloaded with it. It is the #1 ingredient you'll be desperate to reduce if you want to increase your vitality all day, every day.

8

The slimming industry loves dieters!

Are you one of those people that are constantly on a diet with little or no result? Let me tell you, the diet industry makes billions by keeping you on a diet forever. How? They know sugar causes weight gain and that's why they remove fat from their 'diet' meals and replace it with – yes, you may have guessed – sugar! Don't allow yourself to be duped by savvy marketing that encourages you to buy diet products. They seldom work.

9

Listen to your gut

The gut is often referred to as the second mind, so you might want to tune in to it a bit more. Frequent bloating, wind, indigestion are signs that your digestion needs a helping hand. Persistent problems can be linked to eating too quickly but may also be the result of stress. If your gut is 'talking' too frequently ask yourself 'how can I relax more?'

10

Drink more water

What happens to a plant if you don't water it – it withers away! Did you know your body is 70% water, and you need to be 'watered' too? Tiredness, headaches and fatigue can all be improved by drinking more plain water at regular intervals throughout the day. Even better is alkaline water. Sorry to disappoint you but coffees, teas, fizzy drinks and alcohol don't count!

11

Eat Fats

You may be one of those 'fat averse' people assuming all fat contributes to weight gain. But be aware there is a BIG difference between good fats and bad fats. Fats known as Omegas 3 & 6 are the good guys; these fats are called 'Essential' Fatty Acids for a reason. Why? They positively influence hormonal balance, mind and mood and, believe it or not, can assist weight loss. Find them in oily fish such as salmon, mackerel and pilchards as well as avocado pears, unsalted nuts and seeds such as pumpkin and sunflower seeds.

12

Get balanced

What's your interpretation of a balanced diet? Three food groups make up a balanced diet and these are Proteins, Fats and Carbohydrates. Ideally you need to incorporate all three groups at each mealtime. Now you may not be aware that fruits and vegetables fall under the heading of carbohydrate foods too. Take a look at your daily meals; which group dominates for you? Are you regularly including all three food groups in a balanced way?

13

It's not a crime

RELAX. Life's busy. When was the last time you had some 'you' time without feeling guilty? How about putting some time in your diary to do something for you? Maybe read a good book, take a walk or join Yoga, Qigong, Tai Chi or Meditation class. Perhaps simply take a few deep abdominal breaths and give your body permission to let go of your stress. It is OK to chill. Your body will thank you for some relaxation. Just for the record, watching TV is stimulation not relaxation.

14

When is a calorie not a calorie?

Did you know a calorie of fat is not the same as a calorie of protein, or a calorie of carbohydrate? They all behave differently in the body. Get your head round this and you'll understand why calorie counting and restrictive diets seldom work. Weight management only becomes successful when you make adjustments that fit with your lifestyle to serve the bigger picture of your health and vitality. Calorie counting is seldom the answer.

15

Eat a rainbow

You may have heard of antioxidants but what are they? Antioxidants are compounds found in brightly coloured natural foods such as fruits and vegetables. These compounds are nature's answer to help combat toxins & pollution known as free radicals. Too many free radicals can increase vulnerability to illness and disease and lessen your ability to handle stress. It makes sense to incorporate as many colourful natural foods as possible.

16

Don't eat plastic

Well it sounds obvious doesn't it? But beware; you may be unwittingly eating plastic simply by microwaving your meals. Microwaved food alters the molecular composition of food and microwaving food straight from plastic containers can mean you end up eating plastic too. Yuk! Not a healthy option. Oven cooking, grilling and steaming are preferable to microwaving.

17

The skin is the body's biggest absorptive organ

Did you know what goes on your skin also gets in your body? Magnesium is an essential mineral which helps you relax. It's used up in vast quantities when you feel stressed. An easy way of getting more magnesium in the body is simply by having an Epsom salts bath. Buy Epsom salts (magnesium sulphate) from your pharmacy; put a large mugful into a warm bath, lie back and allow the tension to float away.

18

Lose attachment to Good and Bad

Do you often refer to some foods as 'good' and some 'bad'? Start by letting go of any negative beliefs you may have attached to food. If you maintain beliefs about 'bad' foods you'll unwittingly and steadily put yourself in a place of emotional torture about food. Remind yourself 'no food is either good or bad; it's just that some foods are better.'

LIZ KEANEY

Chapter 2

<u>BE KIND TO YOUR MIND.</u>

Life doesn't just happen. Let me help you understand that your brain is not the same as your mind. Your mind (the subconscious element) is the master controller of your life. Life is the outcome of your thoughts and actions. Be ultra kind with those thoughts and deeds feed your mind.

19

Get out red lipstick; not just for your lips!

Be aware; notice the little voice in your head. The one that tries to sabotage almost everything you want to do. It's the one that says 'you're not good enough/worthy/capable enough'. The one that says 'you're too old/too young too fat/too thin' and the one that says 'but' and 'I can't' a bit too often. Listen to your little voice and ask yourself 'Where did the belief that I am not good enough/worthy/capable etc come from'. Then how about taking an imaginary red lipstick and drawing a big red cross right through your belief and replacing that belief with a more empowering one.

All change starts with belief.
'Whether you think you can, or think you can't – you're probably right' Henry Ford quotation.

20

Make promises

Let's start by making some promises. Almost all personal development programmes refer to goal setting, but how about making promises to you instead? You are far more likely to keep to promises. Choose a nice journal and write yourself some promises. Writing helps imprint your promises in your subconscious mind. If you could make any promise to yourself what would it be? Brain dump and see what happens.

21

Get perspective

Don't sweat the small stuff. Does it really matter that you haven't cleaned the bathroom? Does it really matter that you still have 135 unanswered emails? No one ever died as a result. Ask yourself in 5 days time, 5 months' time or in 5 years time will this really be a huge problem. Usually it won't. Think of the bigger picture. Stop beating yourself up about things that are inconsequential.

22

Know there always is a solution

Life wouldn't be life if it didn't give us challenges. Believe there is always a solution and you will find it. Don't be too proud to ask for help. Ask a friend, colleague, family or select a coach or mentor to help you. Remind yourself 'No man is an island' everyone needs support or a guiding hand at times. It's not weak or vulnerable to ask for help. Two heads are always better than one. The most successful and inspirational people always employ coaches and mentors.

23

Stop measuring

Why do you measure your looks, wealth and success against others? You are unique; you always have been and always will be good enough. You can have huge aspirations but do it in a way that recognises your worth rather than compares and criticises you. We are all different. Life is not a competition.

24

Have a clear vision and an affirmation

In your mind's eye, do you know what your ideal body image is? In your mind's eye what is your ideal picture of health or success? How will you know when you've achieved your 'ideal'? How will that make you feel? Your subconscious mind plays a huge part in the end result so be specific. If you simply say 'I want to lose weight' your sub conscious mind won't know if that means one pound or 12 pounds. Get clear. If you feel challenged by physical discomfort or illness in your body, get clear; affirm what it is that you really want. For example, don't say 'I want to be rid of this pain in my back' instead affirm 'I stand with ease and comfort'. Always say your affirmations in the present tense.

25

Stop blaming

Listen to how often you blame others for your lot in life. Quite simply, blame takes away your power to change things. Once you start taking responsibility for your own life everything changes. You will start to feel empowered and you'll notice those who constantly blame others play small in their life. They have a victim mentality. People subconsciously steer themselves away from victim mentality people. They are energy suckers. Are you a Victor or Victim?

26

Measure your successes

It may seem arrogant at first but let me encourage you to recognise your successes - not your failures. Write down one thing every day that you can be proud of – even if it is simply that you got out of bed.

27

Let go of your need to be perfect

What is perfect anyway? Nothing is perfect and that is what makes you unique. Embrace your uniqueness. Breathe a deep sigh of relief. No one is perfect; there was never any need to be perfect. We don't need to try and be something we are not. Being happy doesn't mean everything is perfect. It means you've decided to look beyond yours and other people's imperfections.

28

Just do it

Stop procrastinating; stop making excuses about changing things in your life. Here's the thing; you don't have to have it all figured out to take the first step. As the saying goes 'take one step and you will see the stairs'. Remember, as a toddler you didn't learn to walk in one day – be patient, but at least take the first step.

29

Be grateful

Write down at least three things to be grateful for every day. If you start being mindful of gratitude you'll start radiating an empowering and magnetising vibration that says I'm worthy. Your vibration will help attract other vibrant, energetic and positive people to you.

30

It's never too late

We are always evolving. If your life has not gone to plan so far, and all the happy endings belong to other people why not try a new beginning instead. What can you do today that signifies a small change for a new start for you?

31

You always have enough time

The days and weeks fly by don't they? Time is a precious commodity. Remind and affirm frequently 'I always have enough time'. See how much more you get done and notice how much more frequently you are on time.

32

Just 3 things

How long is your to-do list? Are you feeling overwhelmed by the amount of things you need to get done? Try listing just three things that really must be must get done today. Sounds obvious but put the most important as #1. Do #1 and then reprioritise. Only ever have 3 things on your main list. This way you'll achieve more and feel less overwhelmed.

33

Pretend you are a child

Up until the age of seven almost anything seemed possible. What changed? You grew up and the world became a place of 'don't,' 'can't' and 'fear'. You allowed any dreams to fade.

So how about attempting to engage with the 'child like you' and start dreaming BIG again. Visualise what it is you truly want in life; make the dream bigger, bolder and more colourful. Have a dreams book or dreams board. Write it down draw it or cut pictures out of magazines. Play with your dreams, be creative – let your imagination run wild like a child. If you can visualise it, your subconscious mind will help it manifest. How will achieving your dream make you feel? Breathe that feeling in to your body. All successful people know the power of doing this.

34

Focus on what you can do

Turn your attention away from what you can't do. Remind yourself of all the things you can do and congratulate yourself. If praising yourself seems strange simply start with the small things. Congratulate yourself - you can see, hear, write, walk, brush your hair, clean your teeth, iron your shirt, do your shopping...and the list goes on. Then turn your attention to what you do want to do in life. Thing BIG.

35

One state

You cannot have more than one mental or emotional state at the same time. So for example you cannot feel unconfident and confident at the same time. In the same way you cannot be dull and vibrant at the same time. If you had to choose which would you be? Know that the support of the Universe is behind the state that you want to be. Affirm which it is you want to be. You can only be one state.

Chapter 3

<u>BE KIND TO YOUR SOUL</u>

Who are you really? At the very core of you is your Soul; know you are here for a reason, let that reason unfold. Don't allow yourself to be one of the majority that reaches the end of your life without having 'sung your song'. You have values and you have a purpose. This is your legacy. Connect with your values and purpose. Through this recognise that we are all connected and see what unravels.

36

Every day is a miracle

The earth spins on its own axis at 360 degrees every twenty four hours. It's a miracle!! Perhaps you forgot you are one too? Einstein said *'There are only two ways to live your life; as though life is a miracle or life is not'*. Live each day as though it's your last. Enough said.

37

Start every day with gratitude

It's worth repeating again. How grateful are you? Not just for the big things but for the smallest things in life. Remind yourself how much you have and be thankful as soon as you open your eyes in the morning. This will help change your energy vibration straight away. It will help shift your mindset from another day of misery, suffering and mediocrity to one where you can start to anticipate the great things the day has to offer. As your vibration changes so will the vibration of the people you interact with. You will start to magnetise positive and helpful people in your life.

38
Smile ☺

It brightens everyone's day. Look in a stranger's eyes and smile. We all want to feel connected. You have no idea what value your smile may make to someone who is lonely or isolated.

39
Wear an invisible cloak

Your soul wants to be vibrant and magnetic. In your mind eye wear a cloak around you that deflects other peoples moaning, negativity and disempowering behaviours. Let the cloak envelop you in positivity all day, every day. Give your imaginary cloak a magnificent colour or multiple colours – make sure you're wearing it every time you step out of your front door.

40

A most unhelpful word

Make 'Sorry' your least used word. You probably say it scores of times a day even when it's not your fault. If it genuinely is your fault then apologise with heartfelt meaning - otherwise ditch the word. Why? Using 'sorry' imprints a message to your subconscious telling you that you are guilty about stuff that is not yours to be guilty about.

41

Make peace with your past

Write a peace diary – think of all the events and people that made you feel less, inadequate, shameful, lonely, angry and sad. Write the occasions down and send forgiveness to those people that made you feel less. If you can't forgive what happened then attempt to accept they had their reasons for doing what they did and say 'I accept that 'and let it go. Put your thoughts in a balloon and let it go. Holding on to these emotions serves no useful purpose. Accepting is not the same as agreeing. Holding on to resentment and anger is a toxin in the body. Let go.

42

A special day

Make your soul feel special every day. Don't hoard things or wait for special occasions – today is that day. Wear your special dress, shoes, jewellery. Use your best tableware. Celebrate. Why? Because you can, today is a GREAT day!

43

Always discern your truth

If this concept is new to you, ask yourself how does this person or situation make me feel? Trust that your first answer is your right answer. It's called intuition, it comes from your heart. Your heart is the true driver of your life. Don't allow your rational mind to override your heart's desire.

44

Have fun

Don't take life or yourself too seriously. Find ways to laugh even when things are a challenge. Watch a funny DVD or be around children. They always make you laugh. Laughter is its own medicine.

45

Get rid of stuff

Give away or chuck out everything that no longer serves you, isn't beautiful or gives you joy. Clearing out is therapeutic, soothing to the soul and makes room for something new. Give your stuff to charity, 'swish' your clothes at a ladies evening or put items in the recycle bin. If you haven't used it or worn it in the last twelve months you probably never will. Get rid.

46

Focus on what you do have

not what you don't. You will start to realise how truly abundant your life is. If this is new to you simply write down three things each day that you have and can be grateful for. The Universe will reward your appreciation. It may be shoes on your feet, food in your kitchen or simply connection to those you love. Appreciate what it is you so often take for granted.

47

Lose attachment

to your meaning and judgement behind the words, Right/Wrong, Good/Bad and Perfect/Imperfect. Allow yourself to believe nothing is either right/wrong, good/ bad – it just is. Have a vivid and bold dream for your life but lose attachment to the outcome. Life becomes easier when you do. Accept sometimes the Universe has other bigger and better plans for you.

48

Stop trying to please everyone

Are you a people pleaser? Yes, we all want to be liked but the reality is you will never please everyone. Start by trying to please yourself first. It's not selfish; people will start to respect you more. Start saying 'No' to demands on your time or freedom when you previously may have been tempted to say 'yes'. See what happens. It won't make you a bad person. Odds on you'll start attracting more respect.

49

Don't judge a book by its cover

There is a story behind every person. Think of this before you judge or label people. We all breathe same air, we are all connected. Embrace connection, embrace man and woman-kind. Applaud uniqueness in others especially those that have the courage to stand out and be different. Similarly, don't change so that people will like you. Be yourself, remain the real you. Live your life in accord with your values and the right people will love the real you.

50

Consider your words and actions

Treat others as you would like to be treated, as the saying goes 'love thy neighbour'. What goes around comes around. It's called Karma. Don't seek revenge, if someone has wronged you hand it over to the Universe. The Universe will sort it out all in good time.

51
Stop

and Listen. Listen to the birds, listen to nature and hear the silence. Stop, gaze at the clouds and take yourself out of your busy-ness to connect and immerse yourself in the peace of nature. Allow yourself to really be in that place of peace and tranquillity even if it is only for a few minutes each day.

52
Be caring, compassionate and kind

But recognise it's NOT your responsibility to take on other people's problems. It's their stuff. There is a subtle difference here. You are responsible for your life; they are responsible for theirs. Don't allow your energies to be affected by other people's problems. Lend a hand but also recognise when to let go.

53

Set standards

Your time and freedom are precious. Don't allow yourself to be robbed of them by other people. Set boundaries/standards. For example place a 'Do Not Disturb' note on your door if you need to be uninterrupted both at work and at home. Explain to people why you need to do this and for how long.

54

What is your WHY?

Take a long hard think about what is really important to you? Every time you have to make a decision ask yourself, 'WHY'? Why should I do this? Is this in line with what I value in life? The answers to your 'why' may not always make things easy, but trust that your life will start to flow more easily when you are aware of your values. Your WHY becomes your purpose.

55

Keep your energy vibration high

Surround yourself with positive and uplifting people. The more you do this the greater energy you will have. Other people's positivity will lift you and you in turn will lift their vibration too. You will start to find negative and doubtful people less great to be around. By being in the company of upbeat and positive vibes you will start to recognise more happiness and abundance into your life.

56

A Gift

Life may not always be tied with a bow but nevertheless it always is a gift. A precious gift. Recognise it and share its beauty with others.

57

Lastly,

Change isn't something that happens tomorrow, next week or next year. **'All change starts the moment you decide to change'.**

Thank you for reading this book.

ABOUT THE AUTHOR

Liz Keaney ~ The 'Kindnesscode Warrior' empowers women to step into their **Confidence, Energy and Purpose** to live a life rich in **Health, Joy and Abundance**.

Several years ago a second major health challenge nudged Liz into recognising her life needed changing. Her 'wake *up moment'* saw her embark on a HUGE journey, opening her mind to learn as much as possible to improve her own health and lifestyle in practical and do-able ways.

Experiencing profound effects of nutritional adjustments and energy work she left her corporate job, followed her heart and threw herself into qualifications in **Naturopathic Health, Nutritional Therapy, Mind Body Intuition, Emotional Intelligence, Qigong** and **Energy Medicine**.

Today she puts all this under the label of **'The Kindnesscode'** helping busy, intelligent women get **perspective,** unlock their **C O D E,** discover their **WHY** and transform **Confidence** and **Energy and Purpose** to experience a more fulfilling, joyful and connected life.

Her belief is: All healing starts with **Self Kindness** (not in an arrogant or vain way) but simply with an **awareness** of how you feed your **Body Mind and Soul.**

She is a **Professional Speaker, Coach** and **Media Contributor** facilitating **workshops** and **retreats.** Her work has featured on the radio, in newspapers and magazines and her next book 'Warrior Women' is out soon. She is also the founder of the Kindnesscode Community — a women's empowerment group whose woman-kind is going viral.

If you would like to purchase additional copies of this book please contact Liz Keaney ~ The Kindnesscode Warrior at liz@lizkeaney.co.uk

Please join the other 'Warrior Women' and share feedback on how tips in this book have empowered you to live your life with more Health, Joy and Abundance.

You can email feedback to liz@lizkeaney.co.uk

Or connect with her:

LinkedIn   Liz (Kindnesscode Warrior) Keaney

Twitter   @lizkeaney   #Kindnesscode

Facebook   liz.keaney.9   Kindnesscode Warrior

www.lizkeaney.com

Printed in Great Britain
by Amazon.co.uk, Ltd.,
Marston Gate.